HOW TO SUCK AS A LEADER

A COMPANION WORKBOOK

Your Tactical Guide To Fixing The Top 15 Leadership Mistakes Covered In The Book 'How To Suck As A Leader'

TRAVIS DALRYMPLE

© Copyright 2025 - All rights reserved.

The content contained within this book may not be reproduced, duplicated or transmitted without direct written permission from the author or the publisher. Under no circumstances will any blame or legal responsibility be held against the publisher, or author, for any damages, reparation, or monetary loss due to the information contained within this book, either directly or indirectly.

Legal Notice:
This book is copyright protected. It is only for personal use. You cannot amend, distribute, sell, use, quote or paraphrase any part, or the content within this book, without the consent of the author or publisher.

Disclaimer Notice:
Please note the information contained within this document is for educational and entertainment purposes only. All effort has been executed to present accurate, up to date, reliable, complete information. No warranties of any kind are declared or implied. Readers acknowledge that the author is not engaged in the rendering of legal, financial, medical or professional advice. The content within this book has been derived from various sources. Please consult a licensed professional before attempting any techniques outlined in this book.

By reading this document, the reader agrees that under no circumstances is the author responsible for any losses, direct or indirect, that are incurred as a result of the use of the information contained within this document, including, but not limited to, errors, omissions, or inaccuracies.

HOW TO SUCK AS A LEADER

A COMPANION WORKBOOK

Your Tactical Guide To Fixing The Top 15 Leadership Mistakes Covered In The Book 'How To Suck As A Leader'

TRAVIS DALRYMPLE

WHY I MADE THIS WORKBOOK

Let's be honest—most workbooks are just a sad collection of blank lines, vague questions, and no plan for success.

Aka: They suck.

This one's different. You'll actually use it.
This isn't here to make you feel productive.

It's here to help you become a better leader—one action step at a time.

Each section of this workbook lines up directly with a chapter from *How to Suck as a Leader*.

This Workbook exists for one purpose: To get you to take Action.

A lot of leaders sit around waiting to feel *motivated* before they make a change.

That's a trap.
Motivation doesn't come first.
Action does.

Think about it like cleaning your house.

No one really wants to start. But once you finally get up and wipe down the counter, you suddenly find yourself vacuuming, reorganizing the junk drawer, and scrubbing blinds you forgot existed.

The energy to keep going doesn't show up until *after* you start moving.

Action creates momentum.
Momentum creates motivation.
And that's what leads to real change.

So if you're waiting to feel ready before you start leading differently—don't.

Start doing, even if it's small. The motivation will catch up later.

HOW TO USE THIS WORKBOOK

If you just started or are in the middle of reading How To Suck As A Leader:

I would recommend finishing whatever chapter you're on, then open this Workbook and complete that chapter's respective section.

Then keep going in order. You can return to previous chapters later so you don't have to backtrack.

You'll be creating your own road map to becoming a better leader *throughout the book* instead of at the end. And, more importantly, you can start taking action on those items immediately.

If you finished reading How To Suck As A Leader:

I would recommend starting at the beginning of this workbook and working your way through it in order.

It'll be easy to keep track of your progress and you can knock out a few action items quickly.

If you don't own How To Suck As A Leader:

I have no idea why you're reading this. But I would read the main book first as you'll be missing context.

Once you complete the workbook:

You're going to have a huge list of 57 actions to take to start becoming a better leader immediately.

Don't freak out. Stay calm.

I'll show you how to prioritize them so you don't have a panic attack.
I got you. I'll break down how to handle the list once you get to the end of the workbook.

Having said that, do your thing. Choose your own adventure on how you want to use this.

WHAT'S INSIDE THE WORKBOOK

You'll find:

1. A brief summary of each chapter as a reminder of what you read.

2. Hard questions to make you pause and think. The questions are designed to push you outside your comfort zone and into the person you want to become.

The reason most people don't succeed is because they *don't ask themselves the right questions.* I've done the legwork for you. All you have to do is answer them.

3. Clear, **actionable** steps you can take right now—before your next team meeting, Slack message, or awkward one-on-one.

4. Example Action Steps from my own life to show you how to do it. My answers apply to *me*.

You have to come up with your own specific action items based on the prompts. I'm just showing you what the actions might look or sound like.

This isn't busywork as I have no desire to waste your time.

This is leadership work.

This is the work that most people never do.

But you're not most people.

You're serious about growing your team, your business, or even just yourself—and reading the book is step one.

Doing something with it?

That's what separates the leaders from the bosses.

Let's get to it.

TABLE OF CONTENTS

Preface 1
   The Three Lenses of Leadership 2

Part 1: Owning Your Leadership 4
   Mindset Shift #1: "I'm Not a Leader" 5
   Mindset Shift #2: "There's No Going Back" 7
   Mindset Shift #3: "It's Not My Fault" 9

Part 2: Leading Yourself 12
   Mistake #1: Don't Trust Your Instincts 13
   Mistake #2: Chase Perfection 15
   Mistake #3: Do Everything Yourself 17
   Mistake #4: Ignore Your Health 20
   Mistake #5: Time Management is Overrated 22

Part 3: Leading Others 25
   Mistake #6: Never Ask Questions 26
   Mistake #7: Always Be Available 28
   Mistake #8: Speak First 30
   Mistake #9: Create Confusion Instead of Clarity 32
   Mistake #10: Be As Reactive As Possible 34
   Mistake #11: Avoid Feedback At All Costs 36

Part 4: Leading For the Long Haul 38
   Mistake #12: Stop Learning 39
   Mistake #13: Fun is for Suckers 41
   Mistake #14: Never Take Breaks 43
   Mistake #15: Trust is Pointless 45

What to Do With The Action Items You Created 47
   The Leadership Lab 50

PREFACE

THE THREE LENSES OF LEADERSHIP

THE THREE LENSES OF LEADERSHIP

Summary
This chapter introduces three essential ways to view leadership:

- Skills – Tactical items that you need to improve. They're the how-tos. Time management. Sales calls. Delegating. Running meetings. Giving feedback without sounding like a jerk.

- Character Traits – This is about the kind of leader you're being, not just what you say you're doing.

- Beliefs – They're the internal stories that shape how you show up

Most struggling leaders operate from just one or two lenses—usually stuck in the day-to-day or wrapped up in personal development but neglecting strategy. Great leadership requires zooming in and zooming out regularly between all three lenses.

This chapter reminds you that leadership isn't just about relationships or results—it's about balancing all three lenses without getting tunnel vision.

Hard Questions:

1. What leadership skill am I avoiding practicing because I feel like I should already be good at it?

2. What character trait am I proud of—and which one do I need to level up?

3. Where in my life or business am I plateauing–and what lens explains why?

ACTION STEPS TO TAKE *NOW*

1. Identify one SKILL you need to improve.
Make an action plan to improve that skill, whether through education, mentorship, or outside guidance.

Your SKILL to improve: _____

_____

My example: I used to be terrible at public speaking, which is obviously a core component of leading others. I signed up for an online public speaking course and improved my skills in less than two weeks. Life changing.

2. Identify one CHARACTER TRAIT you want to improve or change.
If you're having trouble, ask your team (or friends/family) which trait they think that you're missing.

Your CHARACTER TRAIT to improve: _____

_____

My example: I used to struggle with being patient, until a mentor helped reframe my mindset around it. I now define patience the way he did, which is "figuring out what to do in the meantime".

3. Identify one BELIEF that's holding you back.
If you're having trouble, ask your team (or friends/family) where they feel like you don't believe in yourself enough. Then use that as a road map to create a new belief.

Your BELIEF holding you back: _____

_____

My example: I used to believe that I could figure out everything myself, meaning that I would wait too long to ask for help. A mentor of mine pointed this out to me and we traced the core belief back to an insecurity that asking for help meant I was weak. Instead, I chose to believe that asking for help is a sign of strength and will get me where I'm going faster than I would on my own.

PART 1

OWNING YOUR LEADERSHIP

PART 1: OWNING YOUR LEADERSHIP

Mindset Shift #1: *"I'm not a leader."*

Summary

Most people don't feel like leaders because they think leadership is something you have to earn—through age, a fancy title, or hitting some invisible level of success. But leadership doesn't start when you get promoted—it starts when you decide to take responsibility.

This chapter challenges you to stop waiting for someone else to crown you and start owning the influence you already have.

You don't need to know everything or lead a huge team. If people look to you—even a little—you're already leading.

The question is: how are you showing up?

Hard Questions:

1. What's one reason I've hesitated to fully embrace my role as a leader?

2. What's the most important quality I bring to my team as a leader, and how can I build on that?

3. What steps can I take to confidently own my identity as a leader moving forward?

ACTION STEPS TO TAKE *NOW*

1. Define leadership in your own words.
Not some LinkedIn-sounding version.

What does real leadership mean to you? _____
_____
_____

My example: Leadership means lifting those up around me while also becoming the best version of myself in the process. Leadership means "going first" so that others may follow in my footsteps. I'm a guide, not a war general.

2. Identify the room where you're already leading.
Is it your family? A project? Your friends? Your clients? Leadership isn't always titled.

Where are people already looking to you for direction? _____
_____
_____

My example: When I used to coach fitness clients in-person, I told them what they needed to hear instead of trying to sugar coat everything.

3. Apply how you're leading from the answer above to your team in at least ONE capacity. Make it simple and easy to implement.

I can apply how I'm already leading to my team by _____
_____
_____

My example: I took that and translated it to my friends, family, and co-workers.

Mindset Shift #2: There's No Going Back

Summary

This chapter is about burning the boats. Once you've decided to lead, you can't un-know what you now know. There's no safe return to the comfort of playing small or pretending leadership isn't your job.

This mindset shift is about choosing forward momentum over fear, and owning the identity of a leader—especially when it gets hard.

Hard Questions:

1. When was the last time I experienced a Threshold Moment as a leader, realizing I couldn't go back to a previous way of thinking?

2. What leadership practices or beliefs have I let go of because I've crossed the threshold into a new way of thinking?

3. How can I remain open to future Threshold Moments in my leadership journey?

ACTION STEPS TO TAKE *NOW*

1. Write a breakup letter to your old identity. Literally write out:
"Dear old me who played small, tried to please everyone, and avoided responsibility..." Then thank them for getting you here—and let them go.

Yes, it sounds ridiculous, but it works and is a stepping stone in the right direction. I've done this multiple times throughout the leadership journey and it's freeing.

Short Example: Dear old me who played small, tried to please everyone, and avoided responsibility...You were just trying to survive. You thought keeping the peace was the same as leading. But now I know better. Thanks for getting me this far—but I'm not leading from fear anymore. You're officially off the team.

Dear old me who played small, tried to please everyone, and avoided responsibility... _____

_____

_____

_____

_____

_____

_____

_____

_____

_____

_____

_____

_____

_____

2. Choose one leader you look up that you want to emulate.
Write out a note on your desk or phone that says "What would [insert the leader you chose] do in this situation?". Use this as your anchor moving forward to help you make decisions.

What would _____ **do in this situation?**

Example: "What would Travis do in this situation?". I personally use Alex or Leila Hormozi when thinking through business problems. (You don't have to know who they are. They're just my example)

Mindset Shift #3: *"It's not my fault."*

Summary

This chapter tackles the dangerous habit of blame. Leadership doesn't mean everything is your fault—but it does mean everything is your responsibility. You might not have caused the problem, but it's still on you to lead through it. Owning what happens under your watch, even when it's messy or unfair, is what separates real leaders from finger-pointers.

Hard Questions:

> 1. Am I taking full responsibility for my team's performance and outcomes, or do I have a tendency to shift the blame?

> 2. How would my life improve if I embraced the mindset that everything is my responsibility?

> 3. What's one recent challenge I faced where I could have taken more ownership?

ACTION STEPS TO TAKE *NOW*

1. What's a situation where something wasn't your fault—but you're still responsible for what happens next? What action can you take anyway?

What's the situation? _____

_____

_____

What action can you take? _____

_____

_____

My example: I once worked for a business that wanted to change the pay for my team without my input. Not my fault, but I still could take ownership of the situation by inserting myself into those conversations. I made multiple different pay structures that were different from those originally presented, without being asked.

2. Call yourself out—gently.
Where in your business or life are you waiting on someone else to fix something? What's **one** step you can take without needing permission? **Do it this week.**

The place in my business or life that I've been waiting for someone else to fix is

_____

_____

_____

My example: I once had a co-worker that constantly called me "Travie" as a nickname. Clearly not my fault, but I choose not to say anything for way too long because I don't enjoy being called that by co-workers (or most people).

So I took ownership of the situation anyway and politely asked them not to do that anymore. Simple, but still effective.

3. Choose radical ownership for 24 hours.
Try this for one day: **Every time something goes wrong, ask…**

"What part of this can I own?" and act on it—without blaming, just solving.

What part of this can I own? _____
_____
_____

What part of this can I own? _____
_____
_____

My example: I used to get frustrated sitting in traffic (no one likes traffic). But there's a difference between letting it drive you insane and owning it.

Instead. I decided "I'm the one that got into the car, and I knew this was a possibility. I created this situation, whether I like it or not.

PART 2

LEADING YOURSELF

PART 2: LEADING YOURSELF

Mistake #1: Don't Trust Your Instincts

Summary

This chapter challenges the idea that logic always trumps intuition. Great leadership often comes from trusting your gut—especially when stakes are high. Ignoring instincts usually means ignoring what you already know to be true.

The goal here is to help you recognize those gut-check moments and stop outsourcing your judgment.

Hard Questions:

> 1. Think about a time when you ignored your gut instinct. What was the outcome, and how might things have been different if you had trusted it? What happened when you **did** trust your gut?

> 2. Think about a time when you trusted your gut instinct. What happened when you **did** trust your gut?

> 3. What patterns, sensations, or feelings do I notice when my instinct is trying to tell me something? How can I become more attuned to that?

ACTION STEPS TO TAKE *NOW*

1. Track one decision this week where you follow your instinct and journal the outcome.

What decision will you follow your instinct this week? _____
_____
_____

My example: I used something minor when I realized I had to work on this. I'd take my bike out in an area of town that I didn't know well while leaving my phone at home. I'd ride around, get lost a bit, then figure out how to get home.

I'd listen to my gut when my brain said "turn left" or "turn right" on the way home, trusting that my gut knew how to get me back. It worked like a charm, even though I had no context on where I was at the time.

2. Identify one area where you've been overthinking and decide to act on your gut feeling today.

One area I've been overthinking, that I'll trust my gut feeling today is
_____
_____

My example: I used to overthink whether I should workout on any given day. Sometimes I need a rest day, but whenever my brain goes "no you need to workout today", I almost immediately get up and go do it. I don't overthink myself into a corner anymore.

3. Create a 3-point list of how your instinct usually shows up (physical feeling, thought, or reaction)
_____
_____

My example: It's a single clear sentence that pops into my brain that tells me exactly what to do and when to do it.

Mistake #2: Chase Perfection

Summary

Chasing perfection keeps leaders stuck. This chapter exposes the paralysis that comes with waiting until everything is 'just right.' Instead, you're encouraged to take imperfect action, get feedback, and keep moving forward. Leadership is about progress, not perfection.

Hard Questions:

1. What project or task am I currently delaying because I'm waiting for it to be "perfect"? What is one small action I can take today to move it forward?

2. When was the last time I embraced imperfection in a project? How did it turn out compared to my expectations?

3. How might aiming for perfection be hindering my progress as a leader?

ACTION STEPS TO TAKE *NOW*

1. Pick one task you've delayed and publish or delegate it today—even if it's not 100%.

What task have you been delaying that you'll publish or delegate TODAY?

_____

_____

My example: I attempted to create the cover art for my book. I made it about 5 minutes before I said "This is dumb. I have no idea what I'm doing. I'm delegating this out."

2. Set a 20-minute timer and take messy action on a task you've been avoiding.

The action I'm taking today: _____

_____

My example: When I first wrote this workbook, I delayed setting up my website for way too long. I knew it was important, but I just really, really didn't want to do it. So after too long, I went online and found someone to set it up for me. It took 5 minutes.

3. Adopt a mindset of "version 1 is better than version none" for your next big decision.

My version 1 of _____ **is better than version none.**

My example: When I first created this workbook, it sucked. It was like every other workbook. But, I still gave it out to a few friends as a test after only a day or two of creating it to see what kind of reaction it received. Messy action wins. Then I came back and was able to tweak it to be way better.

Mistake #3: Do Everything Yourself

Summary

Thinking you have to wear every hat is a fast track to burnout. This chapter dismantles the myth that real leaders do it all, and instead shows why delegation, systems, and trusting your team are essential to sustainable success.

Hard Questions:

> 1. What are three tasks I'm currently doing that someone else could do? What's stopped me from delegating those tasks?

> 2. How can I shift my mindset from "I can do it better" to empowering others to take ownership?

> 3. What's one small task I can delegate this week to free up time for higher-level leadership work?

ACTION STEPS TO TAKE *NOW*

1. Make a list called "Shit I shouldn't be doing". Set a timer to go off every 20 minutes, then write down what you're doing.

My example: When I did this with my coaching business, one of the first things I offloaded was posting social media content on my Instagram stories. I hired someone for $15/hr, and that was their first task. Over time I sent more and more items that "just take a second", but were bogging down my day.

MY SHIT I SHOULDN'T BE DOING LIST

2. The following day, choose ONE of those tasks and delegate it out this week.

The task from my Shit I Shouldn't Be Doing List that I will delegate out this week is _____
_____

My example: In the above example, I started with ONE thing, then added more over time. No need to overdue it when you're first starting out.

3. Document the process or task so your team can repeat without you.

_____
_____
_____
_____

My example: I used Google Docs and screen recording. You can easily do the same. Doesn't have to be perfect. Just needs to be *something*.

Mistake #4: Ignore Your Health

Summary

Burnout isn't a badge of honor. This chapter focuses on how your physical, mental, and emotional health directly impact your ability to lead. If you're falling apart behind the scenes, you can't show up fully for your team. Leadership starts with self-care.

Hard Questions:

1. How am I currently prioritizing (or neglecting) my physical health? How is it impacting my leadership?

2. What's one small, sustainable change I can make to improve my health this week?

3. Am I modeling healthy habits for my team? How might improving my own health inspire others?

ACTION STEPS TO TAKE *NOW*

1. Choose ONE aspect of your health that you *know* you're neglecting.

The area of my health I've been neglecting: _____

_____

My example: I fell off from constant workouts at the start of 2023. I went from 4-5 per week down to 1-2.

2. Create one simple action related to that aspect and put it in your calendar

My action _____

☐ **Add to your calendar**

My example: I decided to meet in the middle and make my goal 3 workouts per week.

3. Track your results so you can see how you're doing.
What gets measured, gets managed.

My example: I build a simple spreadsheet to track my workouts and how I was doing each week. I still, to this day, use that same spreadsheet. Works wonders.

Mistake #5: Time Management is Overrated

Summary

Time management doesn't fix leadership problems—priority management does. This chapter helps you realize that managing your calendar isn't enough; you have to know what actually matters and structure your time around that.

Hard Questions:

> 1. How often do you currently time-block your calendar, and what are the categories of the individual time-blocks?

> 2. What are the biggest distractions that regularly interrupt your work? How can you remove or reduce them to create more focused "deep work" time?

> 3. When was the last time you reviewed your weekly schedule? How could more consistent reflection and planning improve your leadership and overall business progress?

ACTION STEPS TO TAKE *NOW*

1. Write out your non-negotiable commitments (5-10 minutes)

My non-negotiable commitments are: _____
_____
_____

My example: Breakfast, lunch, and dinner were the first on my list when I did this way back when. It might seem silly, but I often skipped those then felt like garbage since I had no energy from not eating.

2. Work backwards by scheduling those items *first*. Then put in your work items in your calendar.

Make a list of what's "big picture" and what's "admin" work or "low energy" work. Schedule in your big picture items first, then fill in low energy work after.

'Big Picture'	'Admin Work'	'Low Energy Work'

My example: For my coaching business, I worked on sales and marketing at the start of the week, then worked on client support and admin at the end of the week. Massive difference in my energy throughout the week just by making that simple adjustment.

3. Make a list of common distractions you experience. Then choose to eliminate ONE of those distractions as a starting point.

My Distractions:

_____   _____
_____   _____
_____   _____
_____   _____
_____   _____
_____   _____

My example: I no longer listen to music with lyrics while working. I usually listen to jazz music… because it's awesome and it's not distracting.

I also have ALL my notifications turned off on all devices. They don't get my attention unless I want them to.

PART 3

LEADING OTHERS

PART 3: LEADING OTHERS

Mistake #6: Never Ask Questions

Summary

Leaders who talk too much and ask too little miss out on what their team actually needs. This chapter flips the script by teaching you how powerful open-ended questions can be in driving clarity, accountability, and connection.

Hard Questions:

1. In my last team interaction, did I spend more time talking or listening? How can I improve that balance?

2. What's one situation this week where I could have asked a better question instead of starting with an assumption?

3. What's one way I can start using "What" or "How" questions to encourage deeper conversations with my team?

ACTION STEPS TO TAKE *NOW*

1. Think of a question that you recently started with "why".
Restructure it to start with "what" or "how" instead.

Restructuring **why** to **what** or **how**: _____

_____

_____

My example: Instead of asking "why did you do it that way?" to a team member, I would ask "So, I saw that you did XYZ when you worked on this.

Tell me more about that. What was your process when you were working on this?" I would use curious tonality when asking that question and it would be on the phone or in-person.

2. During your next conversation, repeat back what's been said.
Do this while having a conversation with a friend or family.

My example: When speaking to friends who's work I'm unfamiliar with. I'll ask them about work, then simply repeat back what they said to make sure I understood correctly. Which often causes them to expand on what they just said.

3. Practice pausing.
During your next conversation, wait 3 seconds before responding to someone when speaking. It's going to feel like a lifetime, but you'll live.

My example: Honestly, this one is straight forward. No example needed.

Mistake #7: Always Be Available

Summary

Being constantly available might feel helpful, but it creates dependency and resentment. This chapter teaches you to step back, set boundaries, and empower your team to solve problems without you. The less you're needed, the better you're leading.

Hard Questions:

1. Am I solving too many problems for my team, or am I giving them the space to find their own solutions?

2. How often do I prioritize setting clear boundaries for myself?

3. How can I respond to my team's questions in a way that encourages them to trust their instincts?

ACTION STEPS TO TAKE *NOW*

1. Try this today when a team member brings a problem to you, respond with:

"What's your gut telling you is the best solution here?

Instead of offering your own fix. Choose one of the three prompts from the book and commit to using it this week.

My example: I alternate between my three prompts.
1. *"So, what's your gut telling you is the best solution here?"*
2. *"Would you say that you're coming to me so that I can solve this problem, to help with solutions, or to vent?"*
3. *"If you were the owner of the business, how would you handle this situation?"*

2. Choose at least one 60-minute block each day where you're intentionally offline or unavailable to your team.

Let them know you'll be back—and trust them to figure it out.

My example: When working in my coaching business, I was unavailable for team questions between 8am-10am because that's when I focused on sales and marketing.

They knew this and would figure things out on their own, or knew that I would get back to them later that day.

3. If you're getting asked the same things repeatedly, document them into a quick FAQ or Slack doc your team can access instead of pinging you every time.

My example: When I had a team of ten, we had a 15 page document loaded with common questions so that they could get the support they needed without asking the team. It was updated every week based on what was happening in the business.

Mistake #8: Speak First

Summary

When you always speak first, you shut down better ideas. This chapter unpacks how silence, curiosity, and strategic restraint help leaders bring out the best in their team—and avoid becoming the know-it-all in the room.

Hard Questions:

1. Do I tend to dominate conversations in meetings, or do I create space for others to contribute ideas?

2. What's one way I can reassure my team next time we face a challenge to encourage them to share their ideas before I offer mine?

3. How can speaking last help me uncover better solutions and build trust within my team?

ACTION STEPS TO TAKE *NOW*

1. Ask your team for input before you speak in your next meeting. Do NOT interrupt them.

My example: When I presented questions at a team meeting, I would purposely make sure everyone had a chance to speak and would consistently ask "what else?" after they finished to make sure they shared everything they wanted to share.

2. Let a team member lead a project or decision you'd usually control.

I will let _____ lead/make a decision on _____

My example: I've given people on my team the ability to run our team meetings as a chance for them to step up, lead first, and then would give them feedback on how they did as the person running the meeting.

3. Create a routine of asking, 'What do you think?' before giving your opinion.

My example: I constantly ask others questions about problems they bring to me so that I can hear what they're thoughts are. This takes 5 seconds, at the most, and will be more eye-opening then you can even imagine.

Mistake #9: Create Confusion Instead of Clarity

Summary

Confused teams don't move—they stall. This chapter is all about clear communication: what needs to be done, why it matters, and how to do it. Clarity beats speed every time when it comes to building trust and momentum.

Hard Questions:

1. Was there a recent situation where my team seemed confused by my instructions? What could I have done differently to communicate more clearly?

2. What's one way I can ensure my team knows not only *what* to do, but also *why* and *how* it needs to be done?

3. How do I currently check for understanding within my team? What can I do to improve this?

ACTION STEPS TO TAKE *NOW*

1. Run your last team communication through the "What, Why, How" filter.

Take one recent Slack message, meeting, or email.

Ask yourself:

Did I clearly explain what needs to be done? **YES** or **NO**

Did I explain why it matters (both logically and emotionally)? **YES** or **NO**

Did I explain how to do it? **YES** or **NO**

If not, rewrite it now.

2. Use this question in your next 1-on-1 or meeting
"What specifically about what I just explained is unclear or confusing?"

3. Slow down before you hit send.
For your next team message, pause for 60 seconds before sending. Reread it and ask: Is this clear enough that no one will have follow-up questions? If not, revise it until it is.

As these are straight forward actions, no examples are required. Just do them.

Mistake #10: Be As Reactive As Possible

Summary

Being reactive makes you unpredictable and unreliable. This chapter helps you shift from reacting to responding—with intention, calm, and clarity. Reactive leadership might feel fast, but it creates chaos. Strategic pause is your superpower.

Hard Questions:

1. How big of an issue is emotional reactivity for me on a scale of 1-10? 10 being the highest and 1 being the lowest. Whatever score you give yourself, think about how to move it <u>one</u> point higher to start. Don't try to suddenly be a 10.

2. Think back to a time when I overreacted as a leader. How did my reaction impact the situation and my team? How could I have responded instead so that the conversation remained productive and positive?

3. When was the last time you paused before reacting to a challenging situation, and how did that affect the outcome? (If you can't think of a time, consider how taking a pause might have changed the results in previous situations.)

ACTION STEPS TO TAKE *NOW*

1. Ask a team member for honest feedback about your leadership.

Ask them, "I'm working on my leadership skills and I need your help. What's a situation where you think I tend to overreact?"

2. Practice the art of the PAUSE during your next conversation, regardless of what the conversation is about.

3. While practicing your pause skills, count to 3 in your head (it will feel like a lifetime, but you'll live).

My example: I started this with friends and family first, as it has lower stakes. So even if I felt weird pausing, it didn't matter.

Mistake #11: Avoid Feedback At All Costs

Summary

Avoiding feedback keeps your team stuck and your culture soft. This chapter reframes feedback as a tool for growth—not conflict—and gives you practical ways to give (and receive) feedback without being a jerk or a coward.

Hard Questions:

1. When was the last time I gave feedback? How did I phrase it, and how did the person respond?

2. THow can I make feedback a regular part of our team culture, even when it's uncomfortable?

3. What's one piece of feedback I've been avoiding giving, and how can I deliver it in a productive way?

ACTION STEPS TO TAKE *NOW*

1. Pick one person to give feedback to this week.

This week I'll give feedback to: _____

My example: When leading a team of ten, I had a tracking system showing when I gave feedback and who I gave it to, so I knew exactly who I was missing each week. By the end of the week, I made sure to give feedback to that team member.

2. Use the 3-part feedback formula from the book to structure your message.

This is an actual feedback conversation I've had:

Part #1: *"Hey John, you were 10 minutes late to the meeting."*

Part #2: "Remember how you told me you wanted to be a Director one day? I feel like being 10 minutes late doesn't align with that goal since Directors are responsible for running their own meetings."

Part #3: "So what can we learn from this?"

3. Put recurring feedback conversations on your calendar going forward.

My example: Like I said above, when I identified who I needed to give feedback to, I would make a note in the calendar invite of their upcoming 1-1 so I had a reminder. Simple and straightforward.

PART 4

LEADING FOR THE LONG HAUL

PART 4: LEADING FOR THE LONG HAUL

Mistake #12: Stop Learning

Summary

Leadership isn't a finish line—it's a process. This chapter warns against becoming stagnant or complacent, and reminds you that if you're not learning, you're falling behind. Great leaders stay curious, stay humble, and stay in student mode.

Hard Questions:

1. What's one skill or area of knowledge I know I need to improve on as a leader? Who can I learn from to grow in that area?

2. Am I surrounding myself with people who challenge and inspire me, or am I stuck in my comfort zone?

3. What's the next step I can take to actively seek out mentorship?

ACTION STEPS TO TAKE *NOW*

1. Plan one small, fun event or celebration for your team this week.

This week, I'll celebrate my team by: _____

My example: When creating my book I spent several weeks learning Amazon Ads.

2. Reach out to a mentor or peer and ask for advice on a challenge.

Who do I need to reach out to/find to help me? _____

3. Share something you're struggling with in a team meeting.

Right now I'm struggling with: _____

My example: During team meetings, I always started the meeting with "How's everyone doing?", but the caveat was they had to actually answer honestly.

If they were having a productive day, they'd say so. If they were having a shitty day, they had to share. And the same applied to me.

Whenever I was having an off day, I openly shared that with the team so they knew that I'm not immune to bad days either.

Mistake #13: Fun is for Suckers

Summary

Fun isn't a distraction—it's a strategy. This chapter shows how laughter, celebration, and lightness build stronger teams, better cultures, and longer retention. Fun isn't the opposite of productivity—it fuels it.

Hard Questions:

1. Do I create a work environment that my team genuinely enjoys? How can I introduce more opportunities for fun without sacrificing productivity?

2. What's an example of a time when fun helped boost team morale or productivity? How can I replicate that?

3. How comfortable am I with showing my team that it's okay to enjoy their work?

ACTION STEPS TO TAKE *NOW*

1. Plan one small, fun event or celebration for your team this week.

This week, I'll celebrate my team by: _____

My example: In one of my companies, we used to have a happy hour where we'd just talk about ideas for the business while having some cocktails. It was lovely and actually quite productive.

2. Find a creative way to recognize someone publicly.

I will publicly recognize _____ **by** _____
_____

My example: I used to "police" our company slack channel, meaning that when people violated one of our slack communication guidelines, I'd drop a funny police gif on their message to call them out.

It reminded them they violated the communication standards, but they would also get a laugh out of it at the same time (along with the rest of the team).

3. Add a recurring 5-minute 'fun moment' to team meetings.

My example: Almost every week I would make sure that someone on my team shared something funny that happened to them recently. Takes a few minutes and everyone has a good time.

Mistake #14: Never Take Breaks

Summary

Rest is not laziness—it's leadership hygiene. This chapter helps you understand why taking breaks isn't a reward, it's a requirement. If you want longevity, clarity, and better decision-making, you've got to pause.

Hard Questions:

1. How often do I take breaks, and how does it impact my productivity and leadership?

2. What signs indicate that I need to take a break, and how can I recognize them sooner in the future?

3. What would I accomplish by taking regular breaks that I can't achieve by constantly working?

ACTION STEPS TO TAKE *NOW*

1. Plan out one short break, even a 20 minute walk, in your calendar.

The short break I'll add to my calendar is: _____

My example: I plan with my dog every workday from around 10:20-10:30am. It's even in my calendar.

2. Plan out one day off within the next 4 weeks.

I will take off on: _____

My example: I made it a habit to golf during the week every few weeks purely to get myself away from the idea that everything would explode if I took a day off. Nothing blew up and everyone survived. You can do the same.

3. Plan out a full vacation (3-7 days) within the next 4 months.

My full vacation will be on the following dates: _____

My example: At least once per year I go on an annual golf vacation where I'm gone for 5-7 days, and at least twice per year I'm on family vacations for the same amount of time.

Schedule them in now and lock them it. It'll force you to figure out how to prepare for them instead of just "wishing you could take time off".

Mistake #15: Trust is Pointless

Summary

Trust isn't just a 'nice to have'—it's the backbone of leadership. This chapter unpacks how trust is built, maintained, and broken, and why every great leader invests in it daily. Without trust, nothing sticks.

Hard Questions:

1. In what areas of my leadership am I not fully transparent with my team?

2. How consistently do I deliver on my promises or expectations?

3. What's one way I can show more vulnerability to my team this week?

ACTION STEPS TO TAKE *NOW*

1. Choose one trust-building action to take this week (e.g., transparency, follow-through, asking for input).

The trust-building action item I'll take this week is _____
_____

My example: I used to ask my team where I could be a better leader at least once per quarter. I created a safe environment where they could answer honestly while knowing they weren't going to get reprimanded.

2. Have a 1-on-1 conversation where your only goal is to listen.

My first 1:1 'listening only conversation' will be on _____
with _____

My example: I've had meetings where I only ask open ended questions and thank the other person for their input.

3. Own a mistake publicly and share what you learned from it.

The mistake I'll share with my team is: _____
_____

My example: I've told my team on numerous occasions how I've made the wrong decisions and owned up to it. I would apologize, get their input on where I could be better. Then we all moved on together.

WHAT TO DO WITH THE ACTION ITEMS YOU CREATED

WHAT TO DO WITH THE ACTION ITEMS YOU CREATED

You made it.

You read the book.

You answered the questions.

And you, hopefully, made a list of the actions you need to take.

As you might have discovered, you have a *shit-ton* of actions on your list.

That's normal.

Next, we're going to take your gigantic list and *narrow it down*.

Do not - I repeat: *do not - attempt to take all of these actions at once.*

You will end up accomplishing nothing because you'll be too overwhelmed.

Instead, make two lists:
- **List #1:** The action items I want to work on the most
    - Start with the top 10

- **List #2:** The action items that are the easiest to knock out quickly
    - Start with the top 10

Once you have that list, look for actions that show up on <u>both</u> lists.

Start with those action items. You can come back to the others later.

Now you'll have a simple roadmap to quickly get you started.

Use those few action items as your starting point to build momentum towards tackling the others on your lists.

Your motivation to knock the remaining list will come from the *actions you take* on your starting list.

Remember:

Action creates momentum.

Keep this process simple, effective, and progressive.

Without action, none of this even matters.

Without action, you just read a book and completed a workbook for no reason and your life stays the same.

Don't be that person.

Choose to take a step forward by starting to be the person you know you want to be.

- Travis

"DON'T SAY THIS, SAY THAT" NEWSLETTER

Using this workbook is an incredible step forward in your leadership journey. But leadership is a daily practice, not a one-time event.

And if you want to keep improving without drowning in theory or motivational noise...

Join my *"Don't Say This, Say That"* Newsletter.

It's a *free*, once-a-week email where I show you how to communicate like a real leader — not a corporate robot.

Each email takes **less than 60 seconds** to read and follows this simple format:

Context: A real leadership situation.

Don't Say This: What most leaders screw up and say

Say That: What to say instead

The Logic: A breakdown of why it works

It's short, tactical, and guaranteed to make you a better communicator by next week.

To join for free go to: travisdalrymple.com/newsletter

or scan the QR code below.

WANT COPIES OF *HOW TO SUCK AS A LEADER* FOR YOUR WHOLE ORGANIZATION?

If you've made it this far, you're clearly serious about becoming a better leader. So here's a question: why not make sure your team grows with you?

Since releasing *How to Suck as a Leader,* hundreds of organizations—from small startups to state departments—have ordered the book in bulk to use as a training tool, onboarding manual, or culture reset.

It's one of the simples (and cheapest) ways to get everyone speaking the same leadership language—and to stop repeating the mistakes you've already fixed.

Here's what happens when you order in bulk:

- **Bulk discounts** to make it easy and cost effective.

- **Free paperback companion workbooks** so your team has practical action steps to follow.

- **Exclusive leadership strategy sessions** with me for organizations that want deeper support.

Bulk orders typically ship within 2-3 weeks depending on the quantity. If you need books faster, the quickest route is to order directly through Amazon for standard delivery.

To learn more or request a bulk order, go to travisdalrymple.com/bulk-orders or scan the QR code below.

Made in the USA
Coppell, TX
20 January 2026

66338160R00033